Exploring
Combe Down

KEITH DALLIMORE

Millstream Books

This book is dedicated to my mother -
Millicent Hillier in her 91st year

Having produced several editions of Exploring Bath, I felt that it was time to produce another 'Exploring' book, on this occasion dealing with an area outside the immediate city. As Combe Down is my home village it made an ideal location for my latest exploration. From the arrival of the Romans to that of the Admiralty (Ministry of Defence) and beyond, I soon realized that there were ample subjects for this book. No doubt there are items which I have not included. These have been omitted either due to lack of space or to a lack of accurate information. For anybody wishing to find out more about Combe Down I have provided a list of Further Reading at the end of the book.

As in previous editions, this book comprises a series of illustrated plates. The map on the back cover locates the areas covered on each plate. In addition I have included in the centre of the book a map showing the sites of the numerous stone workings at Combe Down.

First published 1988, reprinted 1996

Millstream Books,
18 The Tyning,
Bath BA2 6AL

Printed in Great Britain by The Matthews Wright Press Ltd, Chard, Somerset.

ISBN 0948975121

ST. MARTIN'S HOSPITAL, BUILT IN 1838 AS A WORKHOUSE. IT WAS THEN KNOWN AS FROME ROAD HOUSE. THE CHAPEL WAS BUILT IN 1843 BY JOHN PLASS (SEE BELOW) AND DEDICATED TO ST. MARTIN OF TOURS. WHEN THE WORKHOUSE BECAME A HOSPITAL IT WAS RE-NAMED ST. MARTIN'S

TYPICAL SLEEPING ACCOMMODATION FOR INMATES OF A WORKHOUSE

PATRICK ALEXANDER, 1867-1943, PIONEER BALLOONIST, METEOROLOGIST & AERONAUTICAL ENGINEER, WORKED FOR A TIME ON THIS SITE

MIDFORD ROAD

ST. MARTIN'S HOSPITAL

FORMER QUARRY USED AS A DUMPING GROUND FOR THE TRAMS WHEN TAKEN OUT OF SERVICE IN 1939. THEY WERE THEN BROKEN UP FOR SCRAP

ST. MARTIN'S CHURCH

TO RECORD THE SERVICES OF
JOHN PLASS AN INMATE OF
THIS WORKHOUSE WHO AT THE AGE
OF 78 WORKING WITH MUCH ZEAL AND
INDUSTRY LAID ALL THE STONE
OF THIS BUILDING.
DIED 5TH JUNE 1849, AGED 82.
AND IS BURIED IN THE ADJOINING
GROUND

CRANE USED DURING QUARRY WORKING, NOW PRESERVED ON THIS SITE

Plate 1

THESE BUILDINGS WERE ERECTED IN 1939 FOR USE AS A MILITARY HOSPITAL

THE WOUNDED AT THIS HOSPITAL ALL WORE THE SAME TYPE OF UNIFORM – BLUE JACKET, WHITE SHIRT, RED TIE, WITH THEIR 'NORMAL' SERVICE TROUSERS

A GIBBET STOOD NEAR THESE CROSSROADS. ONE MAN IS SAID TO HAVE BEEN HANGED HERE IN 1767

SITE OF 1939-45 WARTIME AUXILIARY FIRE STATION – DEMOLISHED 1985

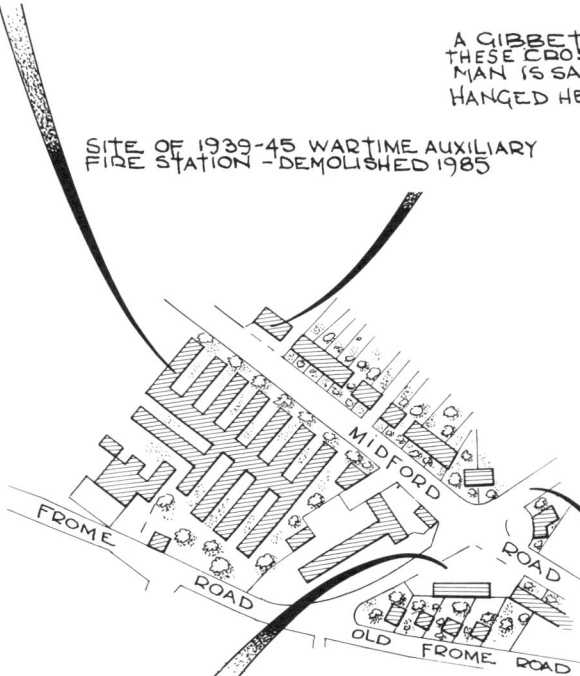

FROME ROAD

MIDFORD ROAD

OLD FROME ROAD

THE WELL KNOWN GLASSHOUSE CAFE ONCE STOOD HERE

y Glaß House

y Croß Keys

2 Mile

ELECTRIC TRAMS RAN ALONG HERE TO THE SHAFT ROAD TERMINUS

PART OF THORPE'S MAP OF 1742 SHOWING THE SITE WHERE A GLASS WORKS ONCE STOOD. THIS AREA IS STILL KNOWN AS 'GLASSHOUSE'

Plate 2

FORMER CITY, COUNTY AND PARISH
BOUNDARY MARKERS
SEE ALSO PLATE 23

SHEPHERD'S WALK, USED AS A
DROVER'S WAY TO AVOID PAYING
TOLLS ON THE TOLL ROAD
(BRADFORD ROAD)

THIS FOOTPATH FOLLOWS THE
ROUTE OF THE WANSDYKE—
BUILT FOR DEMARCATION AND
FORTIFICATION IN SAXON TIMES

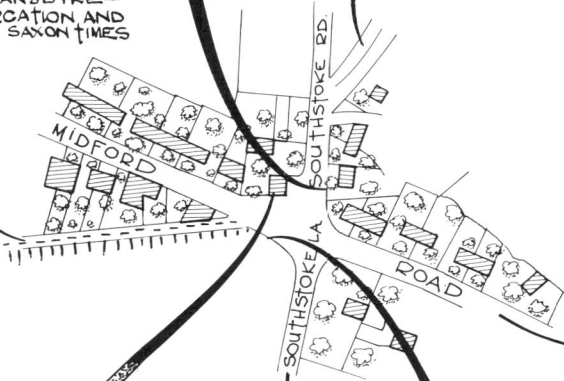

TO MIDFORD

'CROSS KEYS' — FORMER COACHING
INN STANDS ON THE SITE OF THE
ONE TIME WIDCOMBE MANOR

TO SOUTHSTOKE

OLD STONE MOUNTING STEPS
FOR MOUNTING HORSES SITED
OUTSIDE THE CROSS KEYS

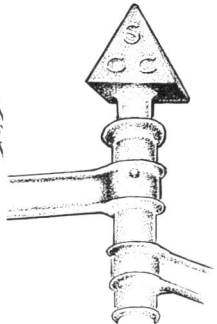

SIGNPOST WITH THE LETTERS—S.C.C.—
SOMERSET COUNTY COUNCIL. THIS
WAS BEFORE BATH CITY COUNCIL
TOOK OVER COMBE DOWN IN 1967
SEE ALSO PLATE 9

Plate 3

ROMAN CATHOLIC CHURCH
OF St PETER & St PAUL
OPENED IN 1965

SITE OF STONE QUARRY FILLED IN
WITH RUBBLE FROM THE BUILDINGS
OF BATH DESTROYED DURING THE
AIR-RAIDS OF 1942

St ANDREW'S, NAMED AFTER
CHURCH BOMBED IN BATH,
WAS OPENED IN 1957 TO
SERVE FOXHILL AS AN
EXTENSION TO HOLY TRINITY

STONE COFFIN FOUND
1936 IN HILL AVENUE

HILL

HAWTHORN GROVE

ENTRY

ROAD

BRADFORD

TELEPHONE EXCHANGE AND THIS
GROUP OF HOUSES BUILT ON THE
SITE OF AN OLD QUARRY

AIR-RAID SIREN OF THE 1939-45 WAR
STILL OPERATIONAL IN AN EMERGENCY

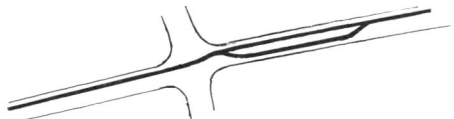

THE SINGLE TRACK TRAMWAY RAN
AS FAR AS SHAFT ROAD. TO ALLOW
THE TRAMS TO PASS EACH OTHER
'PASSING LOOPS' WERE SITUATED
AT VARIOUS POINTS ALONG THE TRACK.
ONE OF THESE LOOPS WAS SITUATED
NEAR THIS CROSS ROADS

Plate 4

THIS IS A TYPICAL DESIGN OF A PRE-FAB, THE FOXHILL DESIGN HAD A FLAT ROOF

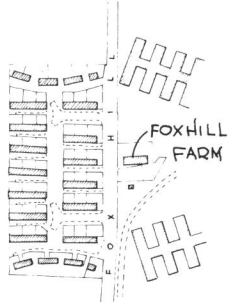

FOXHILL FARM

ON THIS SITE STOOD A GROUP OF PRE-FABRICATED HOUSES, KNOWN AS 'PRE-FABS', THEY WERE BUILT TO EASE THE HOUSING SHORTAGE AFTER THE 1939-45 WAR

TAKEN FROM A MAP OF 1952 SHOWING THE PRE-FAB SITE. ALSO SHOWN IS THE FORMER FOXHILL FARM, DEMOLISHED IN THE EARLY 1980s

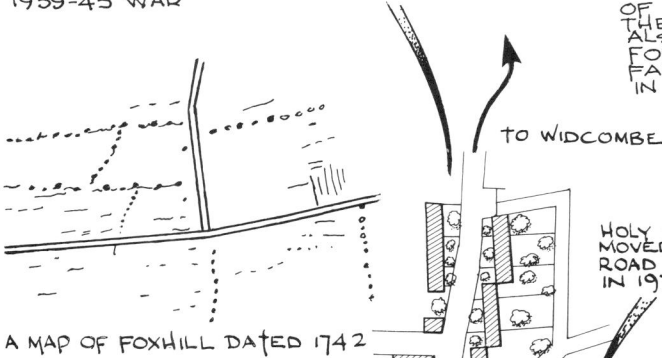

TO WIDCOMBE

HOLY TRINITY VICARAGE MOVED TO Nº 141, BRADFORD ROAD FROM CHURCH ROAD IN 1974

A MAP OF FOXHILL DATED 1742

Stone Quarry

FOX HILL

BRADFORD ROAD

CLEVEDALE RD

A MAP OF THE SAME AREA DATED 1893

GERMAN PRISONERS OF WAR WITH THEIR DISTINCTIVE COLOURED PATCHES ON THE BACK OF THEIR UNIFORMS, HELPED IN THE CONSTRUCTION OF THIS CONCRETE WALL. THE RAISED GROUND FROM THE FLATS WAS ADDED MUCH LATER, AT THE TIME THE FLATS WERE BUILT

Plate 5

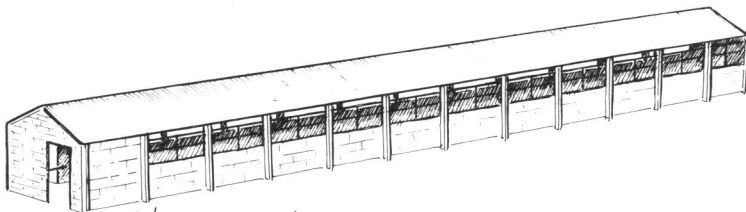

THE BUS SHELTER BUILT IN 1939 FOR THE USE OF THE THEN 'ADMIRALTY OFFICE WORKERS'. IN THOSE DAYS THERE WERE FEW CARS ON THE ROADS, AND MOST TRAVELLED BY BUS. THIS SHELTER USED TO BE OVERFLOWING DURING THE RUSH HOUR. IT WAS DEMOLISHED IN 1986 BEING REPLACED BY THE SMALLER ALUMINIUM SHELTER

THIS METAL PLATE IN THE PAVEMENT IS A TRAPDOOR LEADING INTO THE CELLAR FOR THE DELIVERY OF COAL. THE 'DOOR' WAS LIFTED & THE SACK OF COAL WAS THEN TIPPED INTO THE CELLAR

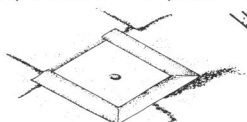

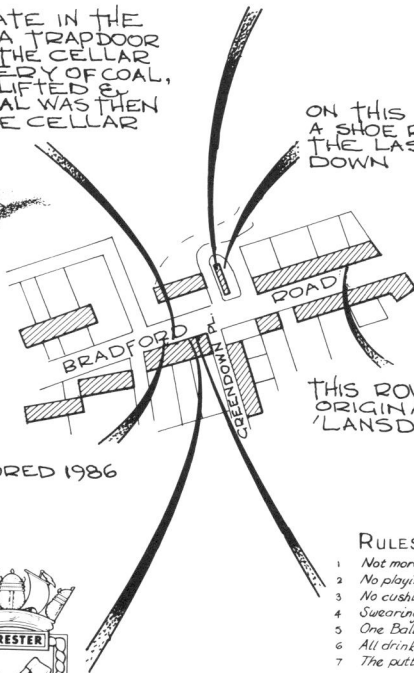

ON THIS SITE ONCE STOOD A SHOE REPAIRING SHOP – THE LAST ONE ON COMBE DOWN

BRADFORD ROAD

CREENDOWN

THIS ROW OF HOUSES WAS ORIGINALLY KNOWN AS 'LANSDOWN VIEW'

RAILINGS RESTORED 1986

RULES OF THIS ALLEY

1. Not more than Four a side to play the rub.
2. No playing off when others are waiting to play.
3. No cushing allowed.
4. Swearing and Betting strictly prohibited.
5. One Ball for each Tie.
6. All drinks to be paid for on delivery.
7. The putter up to be paid One Penny.

NOTICE. That all these Rules be strictly adhered to.

FORESTER

AUDAX POTENTES CAEDO

THESE RULES OF THE GAME WERE FOUND SOME YEARS AGO IN THE CELLARS BELOW THIS 'PUB'. THE BOARD HAS SINCE BEEN RESTORED AND IS NOW ON DISPLAY IN THE DINING AREA (ALLEY)

THIS PUB SIGN DEPICTS THE BADGE OF H.M.S. FORESTER, A DESTROYER OF THE '1939-45 WAR', BUILT IN 1934. THE LATIN MOTTO: AUDAX POTENTES CAEDO. — 'BOLDLY I CUT DOWN THE MIGHTY'.

AT THE TIME OF RALPH ALLEN, MOST OF COMBE DOWN WAS COVERED WITH FIR TREES AND SO THERE WAS A NEED FOR FORESTERS

Plate 6

ON THIS ISLAND STOOD A
WELL KNOWN LANDMARK
OF COMBE DOWN, THE
WATER TOWER THAT
SUPPLIED THE VILLAGE
WITH ITS WATER SUPPLY
THROUGH THE COMBE
DOWN WATER WORKS.
THE 20,000 GALL. TANK
WAS TAKEN OVER IN
1954 BY THE CITY OF BATH
WATER CO. IT WAS TAKEN
OUT OF USE A FEW YEARS
LATER BEING DEMOLISHED
IN 1975

THESE GOVERNMENT OFFICES WERE
BUILT IN 1939 TO ACCOMMODATE THE
STAFF AT THE ADMIRALTY DISPERSED
FROM LONDON. THE ENTRANCES
WERE GUARDED BY NAVAL RATINGS
WITH FIXED BAYONETS AND STOOD
BEHIND COILS OF BARBED WIRE.
THERE WAS ALSO A SENTRY BOX.
THE PRESENT WIRE FENCING IS
OF MORE RECENT TIMES

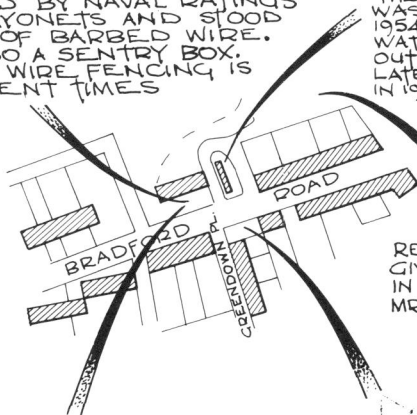

RECREATION GROUND
GIVEN TO COMBE DOWN
IN THE EARLY 1900s BY
MR. LIVINGSTONE RUSSELL

A STONE MINE SHAFT SITED
HERE WAS FILLED IN WHEN
THESE OFFICES WERE BUILT

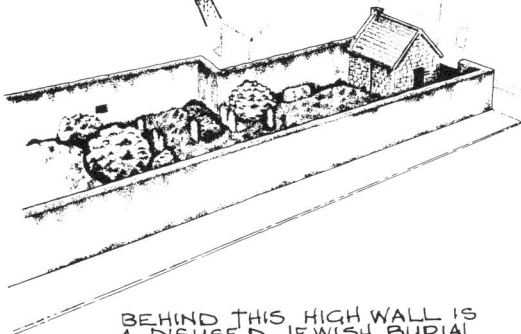

BEHIND THIS HIGH WALL IS
A DISUSED JEWISH BURIAL
GROUND. THERE ARE ABOUT
50 GRAVESTONES. THE LAST
BURIAL TOOK PLACE IN 1942,
THE SMALL BUILDING WAS
USED AS A VESTRY. THERE
WAS A SYNAGOGUE IN BATH
AT ONE TIME, IT WAS SITUATED
IN CORN STREET, BUT BY 1911
IT HAD BECOME DERELICT

Plate 7

COMBE DOWN RUGBY CLUB FORMED IN 1896 BEGAN PLAYING IN THE FIRS FIELD. THE CLUBHOUSE ON THE PRESENT GROUND WAS BUILT IN 1966

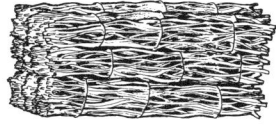

WOODEN FAGGOTS WERE STACKED ON THIS GROUND FOR USE IN THE NEARBY BAKERY FOR HEATING THE OVENS

THE BAKERY CLOSED DOWN SOME YEARS AGO. THE BREAD SHOP CLOSED IN 1987 AND IS NOW A PLUMBER'S BUSINESS

Nº 18 COMBE ROAD WAS USED AS A MANUAL TELEPHONE EXCHANGE FOR 21 YEARS FROM 1906 UNTIL THE NEW AUTOMATIC EXCHANGE WAS BUILT NEARBY

SEE PLATE 25 FOR MAP OF COXES STONE MINE WHICH COVERED MOST OF THIS AREA

BOUNDARY 1912

CITY OF BATH   SOMERSET C C

NORTH ROAD

COMBE ROAD

WESTERLEIGH ROAD

BOUNDARY MARKER INDICATING THE FORMER CITY OF BATH LIMITS. MOST OF COMBE DOWN WAS IN SOMERSET. THE CITY TOOK OVER COMBE DOWN IN 1967

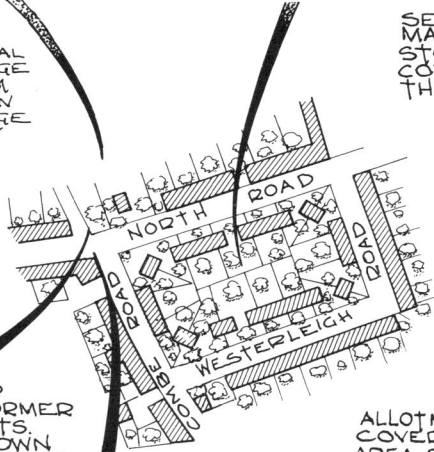

ALLOTMENT GARDENS COVERED MOST OF THIS AREA BEFORE THE FINAL PHASE OF WESTERLEIGH ROAD WAS STARTED

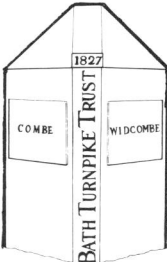

1827

BATH TURNPIKE TRUST

COMBE   WIDCOMBE

THREE AIR SHAFTS WERE SITUATED ON THIS GROUND, SIMILAR TO THOSE THAT WERE IN THE FIRS FIELD

THE TURNPIKE TRUST CAME INTO BEING IN 1827 FOR THE UPKEEP OF THE ROADS. A TOLLGATE WAS ERECTED HERE & A TOLLHOUSE WAS BUILT NEAR THE TOP OF BRASSKNOCKER HILL WHERE PAYMENT WAS MADE, ALTHOUGH THIS CORNER HOUSE DOES LOOK VERY MUCH LIKE A TOLL HOUSE. THE PAYMENT OF THE TOLL WAS PAID AT ONE END OF THE ROAD

THE BUILDING BETWEEN Nºs 14 & 16 WAS AT ONE TIME USED BY THE SALVATION ARMY, IN MORE RECENT YEARS IT HAS BEEN USED BY THE WATER WORKS

Plate 8

1933

FOUNDATION
STONE

1939

THIS BUILDING NOW HOUSES
THE 'NEW CHURCH' BUILT
AS A TELEPHONE EXCHANGE
FOR COMBE DOWN IN 1939.
THE FOUNDATION STONE WAS
LAID IN 1933

N° 26 - FORMER PUB,
THE LICENCING DETAILS
CAN STILL BE SEEN ON THE
FRONT WALL BEHIND THE
PORCH ROOF

SIGNPOST WITH THE
LETTERS - S.C.C -
SOMERSET COUNTY
COUNCIL. THIS WAS
BEFORE BATH CITY
COUNCIL TOOK OVER
COMBE DOWN IN 1967
- SEE ALSO PLATE 3

FORMER GREENGROCER'S
SHOP

COMBE ROAD

ROCK HALL LA

BRUNSWICK PLACE

MR SELLEY'S FISHMONGER
SHOP, CLOSED IN 1973

N° 50 FORMER
POST OFFICE

SITE OF FORMER BREWERY,
ONE TIME SOMERSET COUNTY
COUNCIL DEPOT AND ALSO
1939-45 AIR-RAID DEPOT

ROCKHALL HOUSE, SOMETIMES KNOWN AS
MAGDALEN HOSPITAL, WAS UNTIL 1986
A HOME FOR MENTALLY HANDICAPPED
CHILDREN. IT IS NOW BEING CONVERTED
TO FLATS FOR THE ELDERLY, OPENED IN 1988

KING WILLIAM PUB NAMED
AFTER KING WILLIAM IV
WHO REIGNED FROM 1830-37
HE KNIGHTED SIR PHILIP
NOWELL WHO LIVED IN
NEARBY ROCKHALL

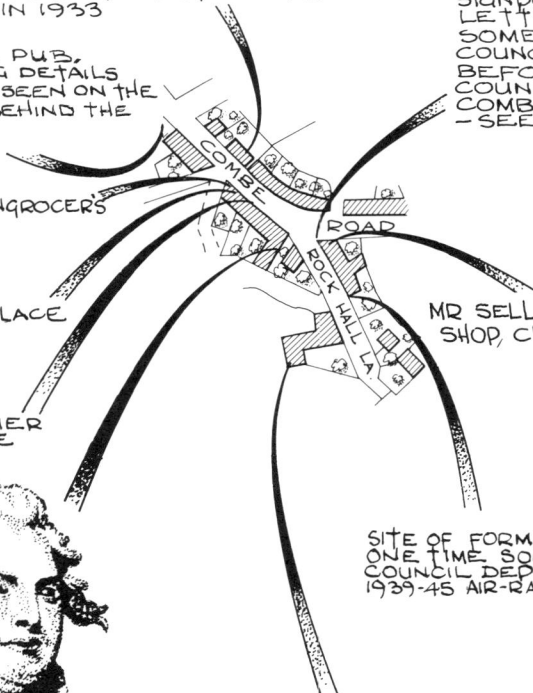

Plate 9

THE END OF MISS ROBBINS
DRAPERS SHOP WHICH WAS
DEMOLISHED IN DEC 1960.
ALSO DEMOLISHED WAS
A ROW OF TERRACED
COTTAGES

THIS ROW OF HOUSES WAS
ORIGINALLY KNOWN AS
WESTBURY AVENUE. AT ONE TIME
TREES LINED THE PAVEMENT

THE POST OFFICE WAS AT ONE
TIME A CHEMIST'S SHOP

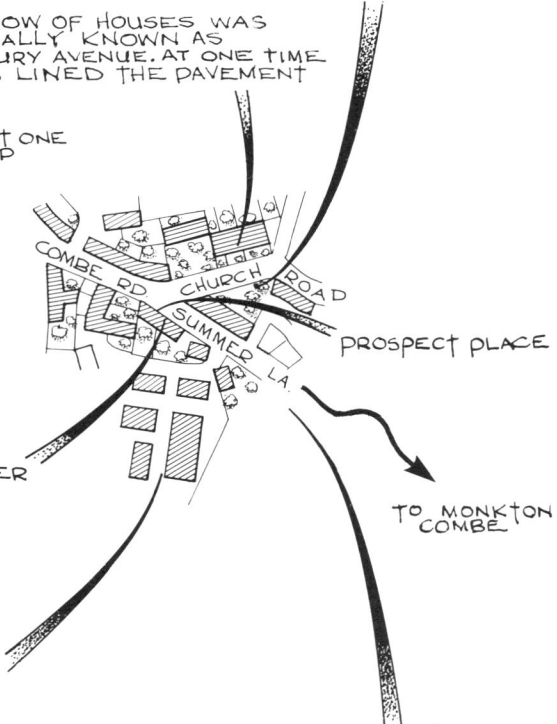

COMBE RD CHURCH ROAD

SUMMER LA.

PROSPECT PLACE

THE FORMER JUPITER
INN

TO MONKTON
COMBE

MUSHROOM FARM OPENED IN 1936

THE ROYAL SMITHFIELD CLUB, FOUNDED
IN 1766 MOVED THEIR OFFICES TO
COMBE DOWN IN 1974

Plate 10

THESE TREES WERE PLANTED BY A MR FARR. FARR'S LANE IS NAMED AFTER HIM

WILLIAM STOWE - A GROUP OF HOUSES BUILT ABOUT 1884, TO PROVIDE COMFORTABLE HOMES FOR COMBE DOWN WORKING MEN. MOST OF THESE HOUSES HAVE A RELIGIOUS TEXT INSCRIBED ON THEIR FRONTAGE. FOR EXAMPLE – LIVINGSTONE LODGE
'HE HAD TO CLEAR A WAY AND CARRY LIGHT TO FAR-OFF HUNDRED LOST IN DARKEST NIGHT AN ARDENT SOUL THAT WAS CONTENT TO DIE FOR PEACE – FOR PROGRESS – FOR HUMANITY. BEHOLD I COME QUICKLY AMEN COME LORD JESUS'

THIS GATE WAS MADE FOR £4.10s.6d (£4.52½p) BY A LOCAL BLACKSMITH

PARK PLACE

FOUNDATION STONE ON HOLM LEIGH – THIS STONE WAS LAID JANUARY 1st 1884 'LAUS DEO'

AVENUE PLACE

ERECTED
IN GRATEFUL REMEMBRANCE OF
THE SIXTY YEARS REIGN
OF
QUEEN VICTORIA
1897
F.G.C.
O.B.

FIRE DESTROYED THE ROOF OF THE CHURCH ROOMS IN 1962. DURING THE RE-BUILDING A FLAT ROOF WAS INCORPORATED INSTEAD OF THE ORIGINAL DESIGN. THE ROOMS WERE RE-OPENED IN 1964

AVENUE HALL BUILT BY CAPT BORLAND IN 1857. BECAME PROPERTY OF THE CHURCH IN 1925, DEDICATED IN 1926 AS 'CHURCH ROOMS'

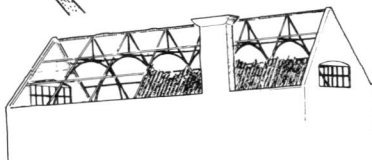

Plate 11

MOST OF THE GROUND UNDER
THE FIRS FIELD IS HONEYCOMBED
WITH THE STONE MINE WORKINGS.

THERE ARE NO COMPLETE MAPS
OF THE WORKINGS AT PRESENT,
BUT IT IS HOPED TO PRODUCE
SOME IN THE NEAR FUTURE

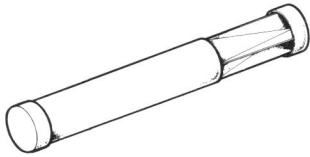

AN INCENDIARY BOMB FELL HERE
IN APRIL 1942

THE PRIVATE HOUSE ON THE
CORNER OF HADLEY ROAD
WAS AT ONE TIME A PREP. SCHOOL

RAILWAY TUNNEL OF THE
FORMER SOMERSET AND
DORSET RAILWAY CLOSED
IN 1966. THE TUNNEL LIES
ABOUT 400 FT. BELOW
GROUND LEVEL

NORTH ROAD KNOWN
LOCALLY AS 'TOP ROAD'

FARRS LANE

NORTH ROAD

THE AVENUE

THE FIRS

THE SCOUT HEAD-
QUARTERS WAS
BUILT IN 1965 ON
THE SITE OF THE
FORMER CHURCH
ARMY BUILDING.
DURING THE 1939-45
WAR THE LATTER
WAS USED AS A
NAAFI FOR THE
ARMY UNIT STATIONED
ON COMBE DOWN

AT THE END OF THE 1939-45
WAR A BONFIRE WAS LIT HERE
TO CELEBRATE THE VICTORY
IN EUROPE (VE DAY. THIS WAS
REPEATED FOR A NUMBER OF
YEARS AFTER. THE CONTINUAL
BURNING OF THE SOIL PRE-
VENTED THE GRASS FROM
GROWING AND THERE IS STILL
A MARK THERE TODAY

ACCESS TO THE FIRS STONE
MINE CAN BE MADE THROUGH
A MANHOLE AT THE REAR OF
THE HADLEY 'ARMS

ORIGINAL SITE OF PLAY AREA

THIS CIRCULAR DEPRESSION IN
THE GROUND HERE MARKS THE
FORMER SITE OF A STATIC WATER
TANK. IT WAS USED AS A WARTIME
EMERGENCY WATER SUPPLY
FOR FIREFIGHTING, IF THE MAIN
WATER SUPPLY WAS CUT OFF

Plate 12

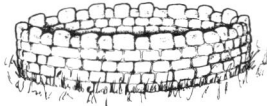

THIS MOUND MARKS THE SITE OF A LIGHT HOLE TO THE STONE MINES BELOW. THERE WAS ANOTHER HOLE WHERE THE LARGE BEECH TREE STANDS. AND ALSO IN THE GROUNDS OF THE SCOUT HEADQUARTERS. A FOURTH HOLE IN THE GARDEN OF THE HADLEY ARMS WAS FILLED IN DURING 1986

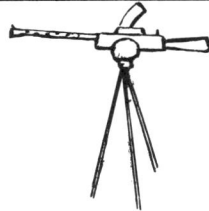

A MACHINE-GUN WAS POSITIONED HERE BY THE ARMY UNIT IN AN ATTEMPT TO SHOOT DOWN A GERMAN DORNIER 17 BOMBER THAT FLEW TOWARDS BATH ON A DAYLIGHT RAID IN 1941 HOPING THAT IT WOULD RETURN — IT DIDN'T!

THIS ROW OF TREES WAS PLANTED TO MARK THE SILVER JUBILEE OF 1977

THIS GROUP OF TREES WAS PLANTED TO COMMEMORATE THE 1937 CORONATION

ROAD

NORTH

THE AVENUE

THE

FIRS

WAR MEMORIAL ERECTED IN 1921 IN MEMORY OF THE FALLEN OF THE 'GREAT WAR' -1914-18 IT IS ALSO A MEMORIAL TO THOSE KILLED IN THE 2nd WORLD WAR -1939-45

THIS LINE OF LIGHT GREEN GRASS INDICATES THE BOUNDARY FENCE OF THE FORMER TENNIS COURTS. THE DISCOLOURING WAS CAUSED BY RAINWATER WASHING THE ZINC COATING FROM THE WIRE NETTING

A MEMORIAL SEAT FOR THE 1935 JUBILEE STOOD BETWEEN THE FLAG POLE AND WAR MEMORIAL AND WAS DESTROYED BY VANDALS. THE CONCRETE BASE WAS REMOVED IN 1987

THE HOUSES OF 'THE FIRS' WERE BUILT AT TWO DIFFERENT PERIODS. A NARROW PASSAGEWAY DIVIDES THE TWO. THE FRONT ELEVATION DESIGNS DO DIFFER SLIGHTLY. ORIGINALLY CALLED RICHARDSON AVENUE IT WAS A CUL-DE-SAC; THAT IS WHY THE ROAD IS NARROWER AT THE AVENUE END

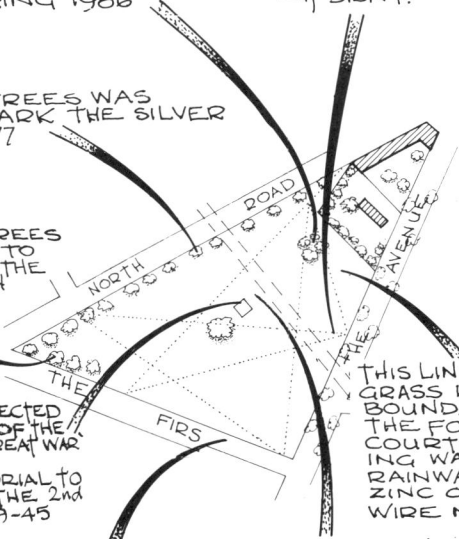

C D W W

G D W W

WATER STOP-COCK COVERS THROUGHOUT COMBE DOWN CAN BE SEEN WITH VARIOUS DESIGNS SUCH AS THESE TWO EARLIER ONES WHEN WATER WAS SUPPLIED TO THE VILLAGE BY THE COMBE DOWN WATER WORKS. WATER IS NOW SUPPLIED BY THE WESSEX WATER AUTHORITY

Plate 13

THIS MAP INDICATES THE NAMES (WHERE KNOWN) AND APPROXIMATE SITING OF THE NUMEROUS STONE WORKINGS AT COMBE DOWN. WITH THE EXCEPTION OF UPPER LAWN QUARRY, SHAFT ROAD, ALL THESE WORKINGS ARE EXTINCT

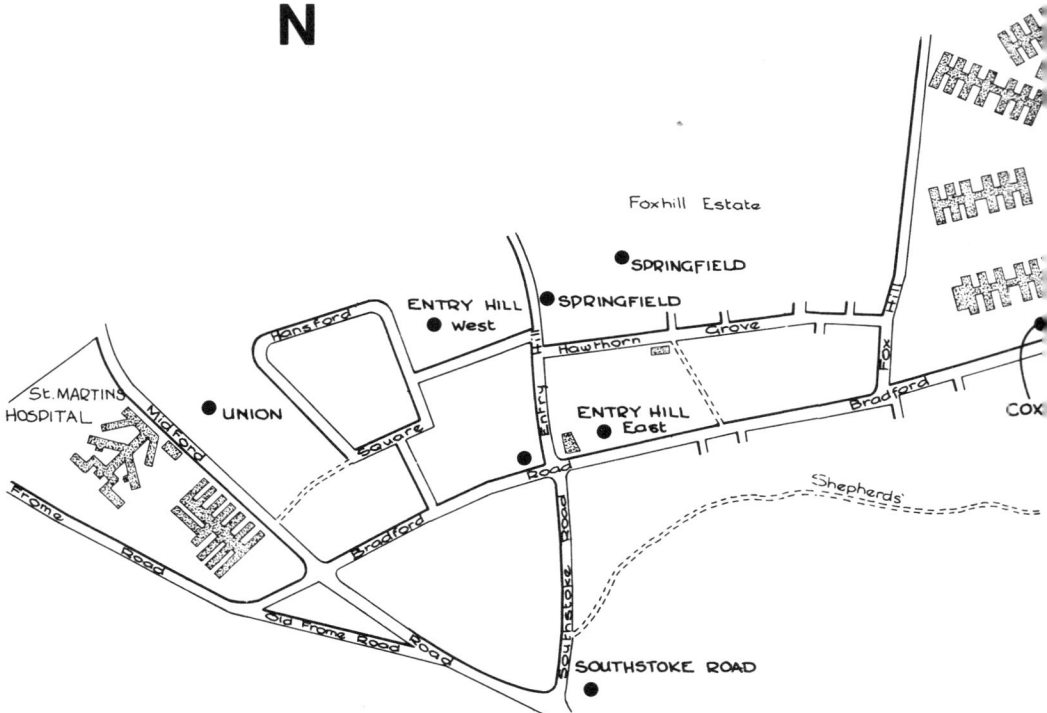

N

Foxhill Estate

SPRINGFIELD

SPRINGFIELD

ENTRY HILL
West

Hawthorn

Grove

Hansford

Fox Hill

St.MARTINS
HOSPITAL

Midford

UNION

Square

ENTRY HILL
East

Bradford

COX

Frome

Road

Bradford

Road

Southstoke

Road

Shepherds

Old Frome Road

Road

SOUTHSTOKE ROAD

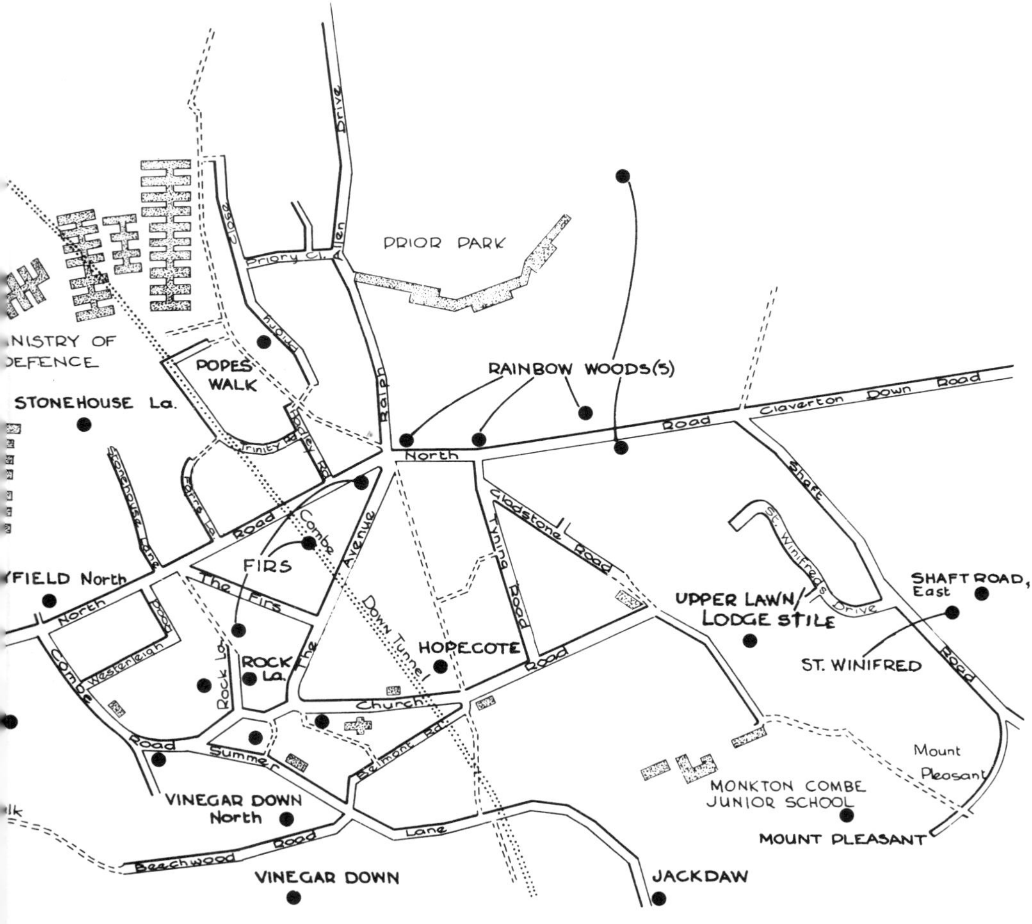

MINISTRY OF
DEFENCE

STONEHOUSE La.

PRIOR PARK

POPES
WALK

RAINBOW WOODS(S)

Claverton Down Road

Road

North

FIELD North

North

FIRS

The Firs

ROCK
La.

Rock La.

HOPECOTE

UPPER LAWN/
LODGE STILE

SHAFT ROAD,
East

ST. WINIFRED

Combe

Road

Westmeigh

Summe

VINEGAR DOWN
North

Lane

Mount
Pleasant

MONKTON COMBE
JUNIOR SCHOOL

MOUNT PLEASANT

Beechwood Road

VINEGAR DOWN

JACKDAW

A SLAUGHTERHOUSE STOOD HERE UNTIL THE COMPLETION OF WESTERLEIGH ROAD. THESE BUILDINGS WERE SITED ON WHAT IS NOW THE BACK GARDEN OF Nº 47 WESTERLEIGH ROAD

DAVIDGES 'PUB' IN DAVIDGES BOTTOM, WAS A POPULAR DRINKING PLACE FOR THE LOCAL QUARRY WORKERS. THE LICENCING 'BOARD' CAN STILL BE SEEN OVER THE DOORWAY

THERE WAS A BREWERY NEARBY WHICH WAS DEMOLISHED MANY YEARS AGO

THESE HOUSES ARE BUILT IN THE HOLLOW OF A DISUSED STONE QUARRY

THE ENTRANCE TO THE FIRS STONE MINE (DISUSED) CAN BE SEEN IN THIS ROCK FACE — A DOORWAY SEALS THE ENTRANCE

CHURCH RD.

ISABELLA HOUSE AND ISABELLA PLACE WERE NAMED AFTER THE THIRD WIFE OF RALPH ALLEN. BUILT ON LAND OWNED BY VISCOUNT HAWARDEN WHO WAS THE HUSBAND OF RALPH ALLEN'S NIECE

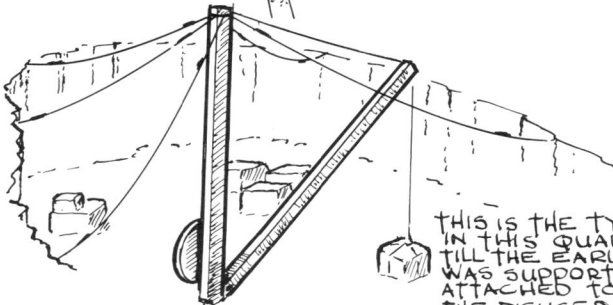

THIS IS THE TYPE OF CRANE USED IN THIS QUARRY IN OPERATION UP TILL THE EARLY 1950s. THE CRANE WAS SUPPORTED BY STEEL ROPES ATTACHED TO THE QUARRY FACE THE DISUSED QUARRY IS NOW OCCUPIED BY SMALL BUSINESS UNITS

Plate 14

THIS STONE was laid by Mrs Gore Langdan OF NEWTON PARK JULY 31st 1888
Carr Glyn Arbroath M.A. VICAR
J F Richardson Maj Gen C^n Churchwardens
J F Ackland
DEO OPTIMO GLORIA.

VICARAGE BUILT IN 1838. THIS BUILDING WAS VACATED IN 1974. THE PRESENT VICARAGE IS NOW AT 141, BRADFORD ROAD

DURING THE 1939-45 WAR THE CELLARS OF THE VICARAGE WERE USED AS AIR-RAID SHELTERS FOR THE CHILDREN OF THE VILLAGE SCHOOL

FOUNDATION STONE FOR THE ENLARGEMENT OF THE CHURCH CAN BE SEEN AT THE EAST END

ALONG THIS FOOTPATH LEADING TO BELMONT ROAD IS A SMALL AREA OF WASTE GROUND. THE PUPILS OF THE NEARBY INFANTS SCHOOL HAVE MADE THIS AREA INTO A NATURE RESERVE

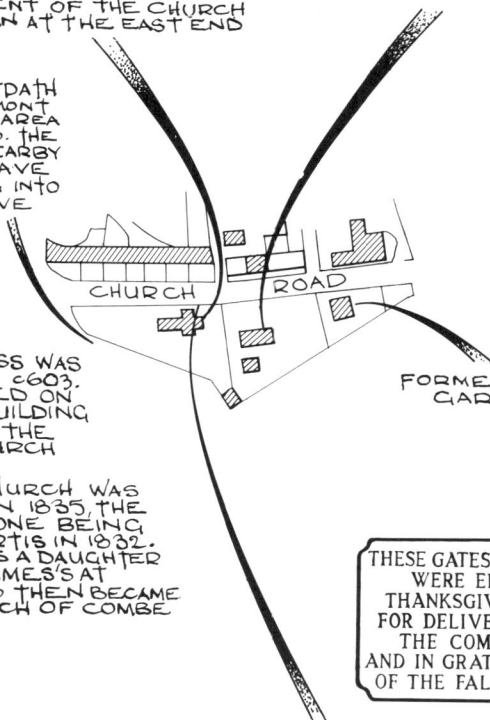

CHURCH ROAD

A GREGORY CROSS WAS ERECTED HERE c603. IT WAS DISCOVERED ON THIS SITE WHEN BUILDING WORK BEGAN ON THE HOLY TRINITY CHURCH

HOLY TRINITY CHURCH WAS CONSECRATED IN 1835, THE FOUNDATION STONE BEING LAID BY MRS PARTIS IN 1832. THE CHURCH WAS A DAUGHTER CHURCH TO ST. JAMES'S AT SOUTHSTOKE AND THEN BECAME THE PARISH CHURCH OF COMBE DOWN IN 1854

FORMER ALLOTMENT GARDENS

THESE GATES AND RAILINGS WERE ERECTED IN THANKSGIVING TO GOD FOR DELIVERANCE FROM THE COMMON PERIL AND IN GRATEFUL MEMORY OF THE FALLEN 1939-45

PLAQUE IS ATTACHED TO ONE OF THE GATE PILLARS AT THE EAST END

THIS VESTRY WAS ERECTED IN 1933 TO THE MEMORY OF ELLEN JULIA HAMBIDGE AND WAS THE GIFT OF HER SISTER MARY HAMBIDGE

THIS PLAQUE CAN BE SEEN INSIDE THE VESTRY

THE UNEVEN MOUNDS IN THE CHURCH GROUNDS ARE SPOIL HEAPS FROM SURROUNDING STONE QUARRIES

Plate 15

THIS SUBTERRANEAN CHAMBER WAS
DISCOVERED IN 1925 WHEN A
SEWER TRENCH WAS BEING DUG
IN CHURCH ROAD OUTSIDE HOPECOTE

UNION CHAPEL
BUILT
AD 1815

CHAPEL BUILT IN 1815, THE SCHOOL WAS
ADDED LATER TO THE RIGHT OF THE
CHAPEL OVER AN EXISTING GRAVEYARD

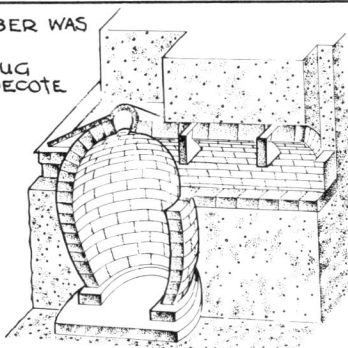

HOPECOTE NOW FLATS
WAS PREVIOUSLY AN
HOTEL BUT WAS BUILT
ORIGINALLY AS THE
PRIVATE RESIDENCE
OF A DR COATES.
ON THIS SITE STOOD
TWO COTTAGES ONE
OF WHICH WAS THE HOME
OF THE REV. T. ANNELY
WHO WAS PASTOR OF
THE CHAPEL 1853-88

DE MONTALT ROAD
NAMED AFTER THE
BARON DE MONTALT
WHO AT ONE TIME
OWNED PRIOR PARK

CHURCH ROAD

FORMERLY DE MONTALT PLACE

FORMERLY DE MONTALT ROAD

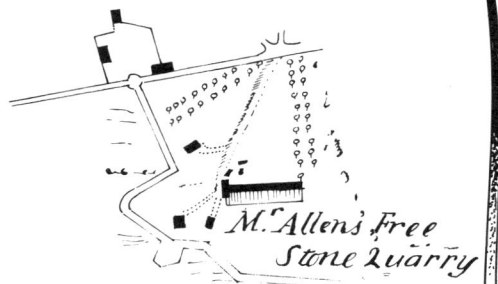

M.ᶜAllen's Free
Stone Quarry

THORPE'S MAP OF 1742 SHOWING
THE ELEVEN COTTAGES

ELEVEN COTTAGES WERE BUILT HERE
IN 1729 FOR RALPH ALLEN'S QUARRY
WORKMEN. DIAL HOUSE WAS SAID TO
BE THE RESIDENCE OF RICHARD JONES,
ALLEN'S FOREMAN. THE UPSTAIRS FRONT
ROOM WAS USED AS A PLACE OF WORSHIP
FOR THE QUARRYMEN

RICHARD JONES, RALPH ALLEN'S
FOREMAN AND CLERK OF WORKS

Plate 16

STONE FROM THIS ONCE HIGH
WALL WAS USED IN THE
CONSTRUCTION OF THE EXTERNAL
WALLS OF THIS HOUSE

GOD SAVE THE KING

ERECTED BY THE INHABITANTS OF COMBE DOWN
TO COMMEMORATE
THE CORONATION OF KING GEORGE V
JUNE 22ND 1911

THE HADLEY ARMS NAMED AFTER
THE HADLEY ESTATE THAT
COVERED MOST OF THIS AREA

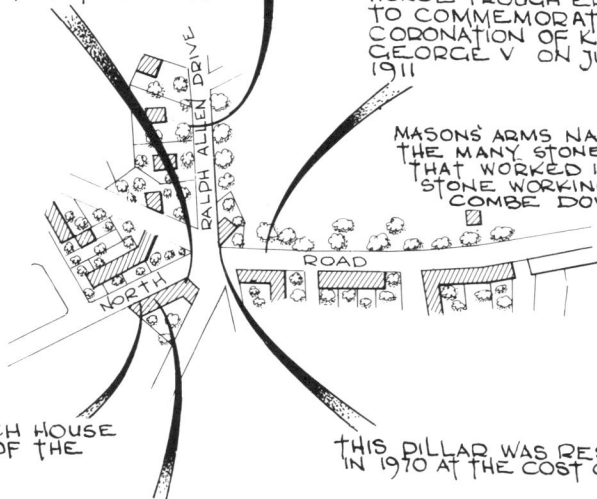

HORSE TROUGH ERECTED
TO COMMEMORATE THE
CORONATION OF KING
GEORGE V ON JUNE 22nd
1911

MASONS' ARMS NAMED AFTER
THE MANY STONEMASONS
THAT WORKED IN THE
STONE WORKINGS OF
COMBE DOWN

RALPH ALLEN DRIVE

NORTH

ROAD

FORMER COACH HOUSE
AND STABLES OF THE
HADLEY ARMS

THIS PILLAR WAS RESTORED
IN 1970 AT THE COST OF £90

VICTORIA ROOMS WERE USED AS
BARRACKS BY THE ARMY UNIT
STATIONED ON COMBE DOWN
DURING THE 1939-45 WAR

NEAR TO THE MASONS' ARMS
WAS THE SITE OF ONE OF
TWO SMITHYS. THE OTHER
WAS SITED IN GLADSTONE
ROAD

AT THE SPOT WHERE THE TELEPHONE
KIOSK NOW STANDS WAS A TRAM/
BUS STOP SHELTER. IT WAS BADLY
DAMAGED BY VANDALS AND WAS
FINALLY REMOVED

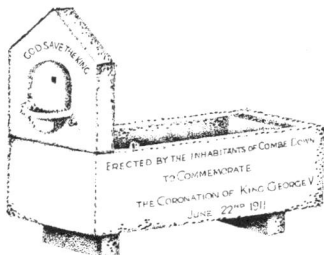

Plate 17

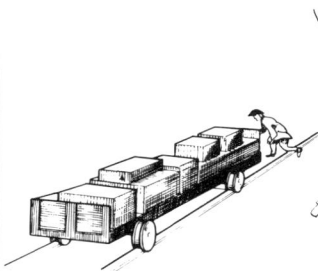

DETAIL OF ONE OF THE WAGGONS USED FOR CONVEYING STONE FROM THE QUARRIES AT COMBE DOWN TO THE QUAYSIDE ON THE RIVER AVON — SEE PLATES 4 & 5

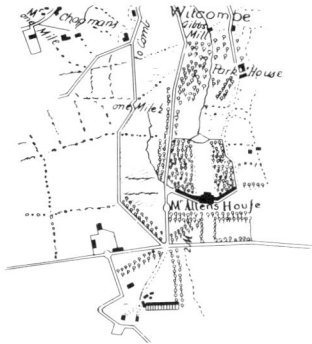

FROM A MAP OF 1742 SHOWING 'MR. ALLEN'S HOUSE' - PRIOR PARK

RALPH ALLEN DRIVE, KNOWN LOCALLY AS 'CARRIAGE DRIVE'

RALPH ALLEN DRIVE

THESE TERRACES ARE PROBABLY THE REMAINS OF MEDIEVAL VINEYARDS

LANCELOT 'CAPABILITY' BROWN, THE FAMOUS LANDSCAPE GARDENER IS SAID TO HAVE CARRIED OUT ALTERATIONS TO THE GROUNDS OF PRIOR PARK AFTER 1750 AND BEFORE ALLEN'S DEATH IN 1764

BOMB CRATER OF 1942 THE BLAST FROM THIS BOMB BLEW OFF ONE OF THE STONE VASES OPPOSITE

SITE OF PRIOR PARK FARM BUILT IN 1747 AND DEMOLISHED IN 1964

THESE TWO PILLARS — THE FORMER ENTRANCE TO PRIOR PARK FARM, ARE EACH MADE FROM ONE PIECE OF STONE. SOLID STONE WITH NO JOINS

PRIOR PARK

THIS LODGE WAS MOVED TO ITS PRESENT SITE FROM ONE OPPOSITE FOR ROAD WIDENING, SEE MAP ON PLATE 20

I 1769

18th CENT GRAFFITO CUT INTO THE RIGHT HAND GATE PILLAR

PART REMAINS OF THE WANSDYKE, A PREHISTORIC FORTIFIED EMBANKMENT

THIS GATE PILLAR WAS MOVED BACK WHEN THE CARRIAGEWAY WAS WIDENED

ROAD

NORTH

AT THE UPPER PART OF THIS LANE CAN BE SEEN THE REMAINS OF AN OLD BRITISH ROAD. THIS LANE WAS USED AS THE MAIN ROUTE FROM COMBE DOWN TO BATH BEFORE RALPH ALLEN DRIVE WAS OPENED TO THE PUBLIC IN THE EARLY 1930s

THESE NARROW PASSAGEWAYS ARE KNOWN LOCALLY AS 'DRUNGS', MOST OF THEM HAVE HIGH WALLS ON EITHER SIDE

Plate 18

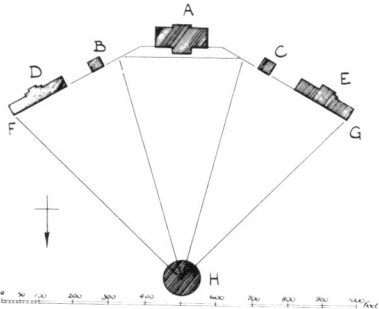

GENERAL PLAN OF HOUSE, AS IT WAS FIRST DESIGNED WITH THE HOUSE A, THE PAVILIONS B AND C, AND THE WINGS D AND E. H WAS THE PROPOSED BASIN OF WATER LOWER DOWN THE VALLEY.

VIEW OF PRIOR PARK WITH THE PALLADIAN BRIDGE IN THE FOREGROUND - FROM A PRINT OF 1858.

STAIRCASE ADDED IN THE 1830s - DESIGNED BY HENRY GOODRIDGE

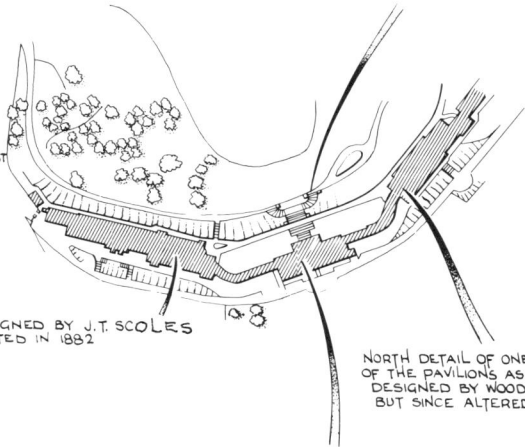

BOTH THE EAST AND WEST WINGS WERE RAISED TO THEIR PRESENT HEIGHTS IN THE EARLY 1830s

CHAPEL DESIGNED BY J.T. SCOLES COMPLETED IN 1882

NORTH DETAIL OF ONE OF THE PAVILIONS AS DESIGNED BY WOOD BUT SINCE ALTERED

GROUND FLOOR PLAN AS ORIGINALLY DRAWN UP BY JOHN WOOD

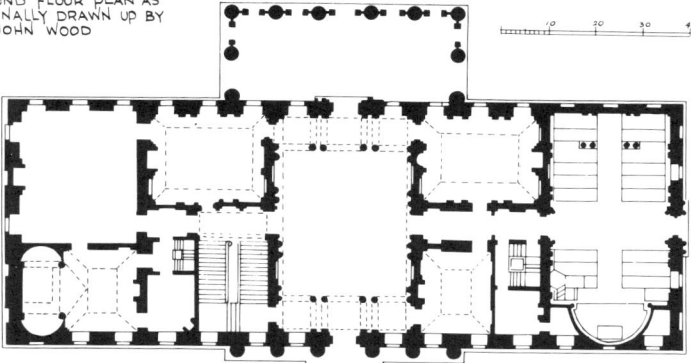

Plate 19

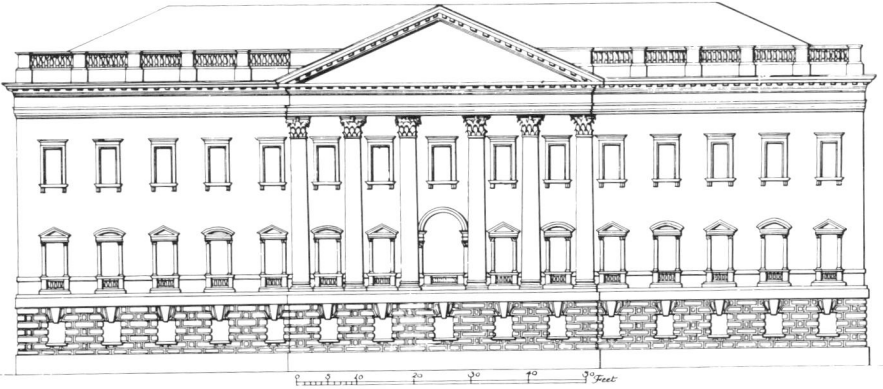

NORTH ELEVATION OF MR. ALLEN'S HOUSE, IN THE 'WIDCOMB OF CAMELODUNUM', NEAR BATH, WITH THE WINDOWS DRESSED ACCORDING TO THE ORIGINAL DESIGN — FROM JOHN WOOD'S 'ESSAY TOWARDS A DESCRIPTION OF BATH' 1749

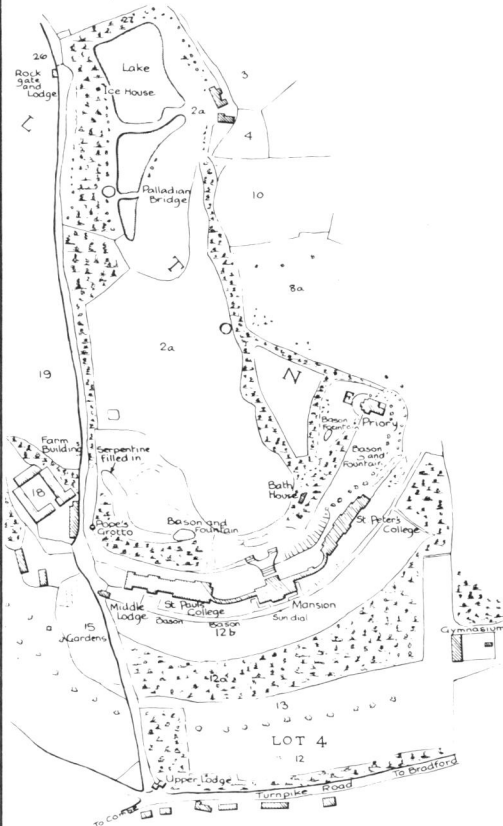

PART OF MAP MARKED OUT AS LOTS FOR PREPARATION OF SALE IN 1856

RALPH ALLEN, FROM A PAINTING BY THOMAS HUDSON 1754

SOME OF RALPH ALLEN'S GUESTS DURING HIS 20 YEARS AT PRIOR PARK WERE
HENRY FIELDING
THOMAS GAINSBOROUGH
DAVID GARRICK
WILLIAM HOARE
ALEXANDER POPE
JAMES QUINN
SAMUEL RICHARDSON
BISHOP WARBURTON

Plate 20

Priorpark Farm

M
P
B
W

THESE CONCRETE POSTS MARK THE BOUNDARY OF THE MINISTRY OF DEFENCE OFFICES. THE LETTERS M.P.B.W. STAND FOR 'MINISTRY OF PUBLIC BUILDINGS AND WORKS'

PRIOR PARK FARM BUILT IN 1747 AND DEMOLISHED IN 1964. THIS MAP DATED 1952 SHOWS THE SITING OF THE BUILDINGS

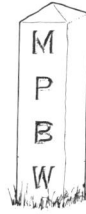

RALPH ALLEN DRIVE

WALL

POPE'S CLOSE

PRIORY

PRIORY CLOSE

BOUNDARY MARKER STONE SEE PLATE 23 FOR A GOOD EXAMPLE

HANGING LAND LANE, ALSO REFERRED TO AS 'POPES WALK' WAS THE ROUTE USED TO ENTER BATH BEFORE RALPH ALLEN DRIVE WAS MADE PUBLIC

WHOSOEVER DRINKETH OF THIS WATER SHALL NOT THIRST BUT WHOSOEVER DRINK SHALL S O

INSCRIPTION ON THE WALL OF THIS DRINKING FOUNTAIN CAN STILL BE PARTLY READ. THE SPRING WAS COVERED OVER SOME YEARS AGO. THE WATER NOW FLOWS UNDER THE ROAD

Plate 21

THIS DERELICT BUILDING SITUATED BEHIND
FREE FIELDS WAS BUILT SOMETIME BETWEEN
1830-40 POSSIBLY FOR THE ADJOINING COLLEGE
AS AN INFIRMARY. IT HAS BEEN SUGGESTED
THAT IT WAS ALSO USED AS A GYMNASIUM

THIS MONUMENT THAT STOOD IN THE
CENTRE OF THE FIELD BEHIND
FREE FIELDS WAS PULLED DOWN
IN 1953. IT WAS A MEMORIAL TO
BISHOP WARBURTON, BISHOP OF
GLOUCESTER. HE MARRIED RALPH
ALLEN'S NIECE AND DIED IN 1779

THE UNEVEN GROUND OF
FREE FIELDS IS FORMED
BY SPOIL HEAPS OF THE
FORMER STONE QUARRIES

Nº 134 WAS AT ONE TIME
A PUB — THE THREE CROWNS

FREE FIELDS
KNOWN LOCALLY
AS RAINBOW WOODS

HIGHBURY
BUILDINGS

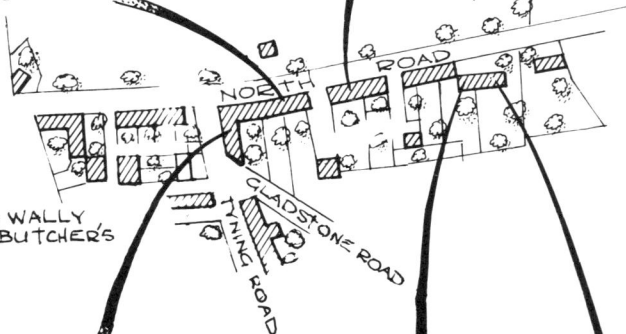

NORTH ROAD

GLADSTONE ROAD

TYNING ROAD

Nº140- WAS WALLY
PEARCE'S BUTCHER'S
SHOP

THE HORSESHOE PUB.
THERE WAS A BLACKSMITHS
FORGE AT THE REAR OF THE
PUB (GLADSTONE ROAD) UP
UNTIL THE 1939-45 WAR.
MR DANIELS WAS THE SMITHY

Nº 164 WAS AT ONE TIME
A DAIRY

THE VILLAGE POLICE STATION
WAS ONCE HOUSED AT Nº 166

Plate 22

ROCKERY TEA GARDENS BUILT IN A DISUSED QUARRY

A No 33 TRAM AT THE SHAFT ROAD TERMINUS

THE LAST TRAM TO LEAVE COMBE DOWN (SHAFT ROAD TERMINUS) WAS THE No 22 WHICH MADE ITS JOURNEY ON SATURDAY 6TH MAY 1939. THE NEXT DAY TRAMS WERE REPLACED BY MOTOR BUSES

P
L AND W
1894

A GOOD EXAMPLE OF A BOUNDARY MARKER STONE DATED 1894 THE LETTERS P L&W STAND FOR 'PARISH OF LYNCOMBE AND WIDCOMBE'

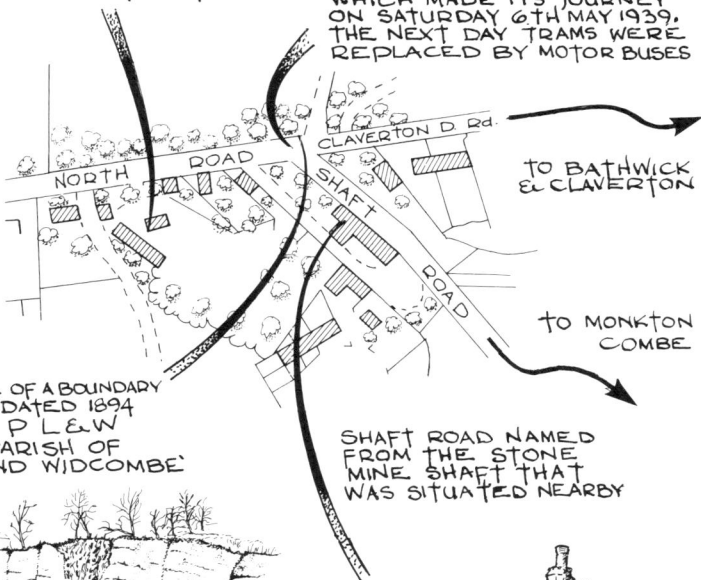

NORTH ROAD

CLAVERTON D. Rd.

SHAFT ROAD

TO BATHWICK & CLAVERTON

TO MONKTON COMBE

SHAFT ROAD NAMED FROM THE STONE MINE SHAFT THAT WAS SITUATED NEARBY

UPPER LAWN QUARRY IS NOW THE ONLY WORKING QUARRY ON COMBE DOWN. THE WORKINGS CAN BE VIEWED FROM THE ADJOINING ALLOTMENT GARDENS

THE HOLIDAY HOME FOR THE DISABLED WAS BUILT ON THE SITE OF THE FORMER CONVALESCENT HOME DESTROYED BY FIRE IN 1971

Plate 23

IN MEMORY
OF THE
Rev. WILLIAM BATCHELLOR
FOR 26 YEARS
A LIBERAL FRIEND TO COMBE DOWN
WHERE HE EXCHANGED
LIFE FOR IMMORTALITY
ON THE 31ST JANUARY 1856
THE MEMORY OF THE JUST IS BLESSED

MONKTON COMBE JUNIOR
SCHOOL CHAPEL WAS
BUILT IN 1893 BUT NOT
AS A CHAPEL. IT HAS HAD
VARIOUS USES BEFORE
BECOMING A CHAPEL IN
THE 1950S

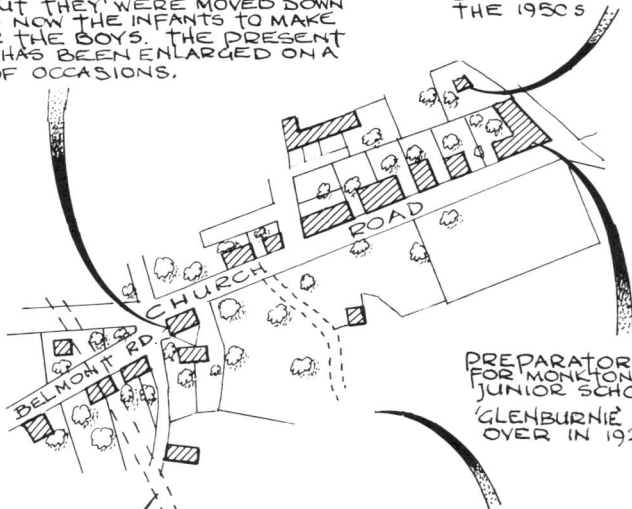

VILLAGE SCHOOL BUILT IN THE 1830s
WITH ONE CLASSROOM AND THE MASTER'S
HOUSE ADJOINING. IT WAS INTENDED FOR
THE SCHOOLING OF THE GIRLS OF THE
VILLAGE BUT THEY WERE MOVED DOWN
TO WHAT IS NOW THE INFANTS TO MAKE
ROOM FOR THE BOYS. THE PRESENT
BUILDING HAS BEEN ENLARGED ON A
NUMBER OF OCCASIONS.

ROAD
CHURCH
BELMONT RD.

PREPARATORY SCHOOL
FOR MONKTON COMBE
JUNIOR SCHOOL,
'GLENBURNIE' WAS TAKEN
OVER IN 1922

SOMERSET & DORSET
RAILWAY TUNNEL (DISUSED)

AIDE TOI ET DIEU T'AIDERA

THE BROW WAS BUILT IN 1834
ON LAND FORMERLY OWNED BY
THE HADLEY FAMILY. IT WAS
THE HOME OF THE DAUBENYS FOR
MANY YEARS. ABOVE IS THEIR
COAT OF ARMS

Plate 24

SITE OF ROMAN VILLA

INFANTS SCHOOL WAS BUILT
IN THE 1830s BUT WAS USED
BY GIRLS WHO MOVED FROM
THE VILLAGE SCHOOL TO MAKE
WAY FOR BOYS

THE WORKINGS OF
JACKDAW QUARRY,
OPPOSITE LAKEVIEW,
ARE SAID TO EXTEND
UNDERGROUND AS
FAR AS THE BROW.
STONE FROM THIS
QUARRY TOGETHER
WITH VINEGAR DOWN
QUARRY WAS USED
IN THE BUILDING OF
THE RAILWAY TUNNEL
IN THE VALLEY BELOW

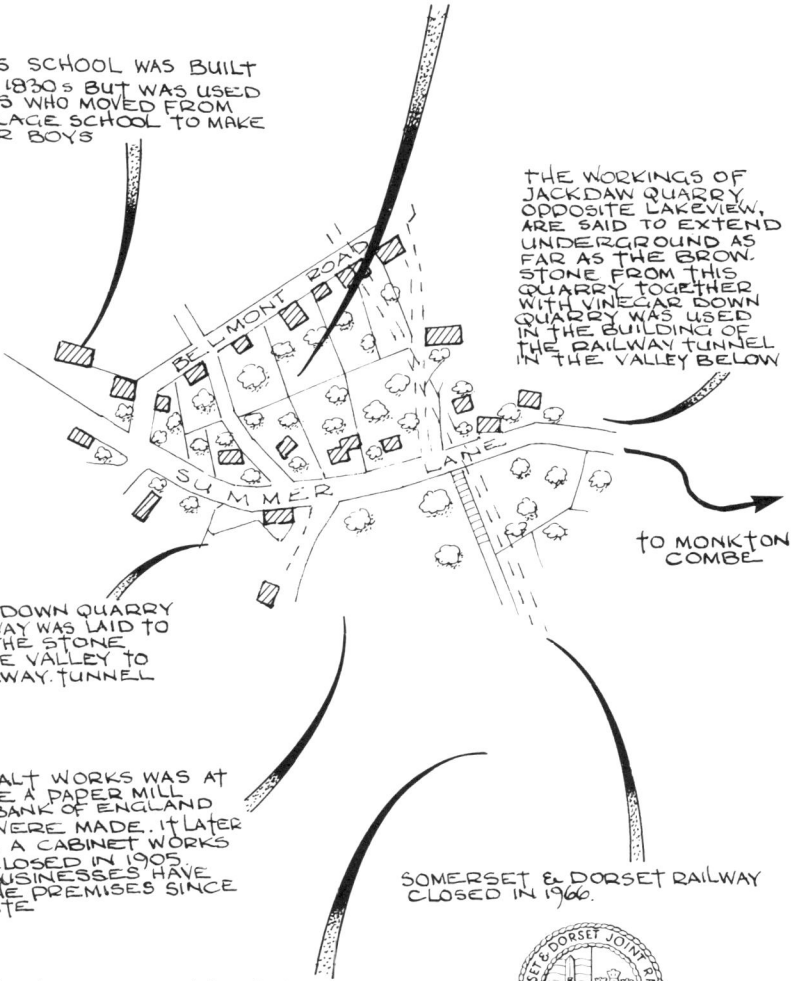

BELMONT ROAD

SUMMER LANE

TO MONKTON
COMBE

VINEGAR DOWN QUARRY
– A TRAMWAY WAS LAID TO
CONVEY THE STONE
DOWN THE VALLEY TO
THE RAILWAY TUNNEL

DE MONTALT WORKS WAS AT
ONE TIME A PAPER MILL
WHERE BANK OF ENGLAND
NOTES WERE MADE. IT LATER
BECAME A CABINET WORKS
WHICH CLOSED IN 1905.
OTHER BUSINESSES HAVE
USED THE PREMISES SINCE
THAT DATE

SOMERSET & DORSET RAILWAY
CLOSED IN 1966.

AT LOWER PART OF THIS VALLEY
IS THE FORMER COMBE DOWN
WATER WORKS. FROM HERE WATER
WAS PUMPED UP TO THE WATER
TOWER ON COMBE DOWN (PLATE 7)
WHICH THEN FED THE VILLAGE.
THE WORKS ARE NOW USED AS A
RESEARCH STATION FOR THE
WESSEX WATER AUTHORITY

SOMERSET & DORSET JOINT RAILWAY

Plate 25

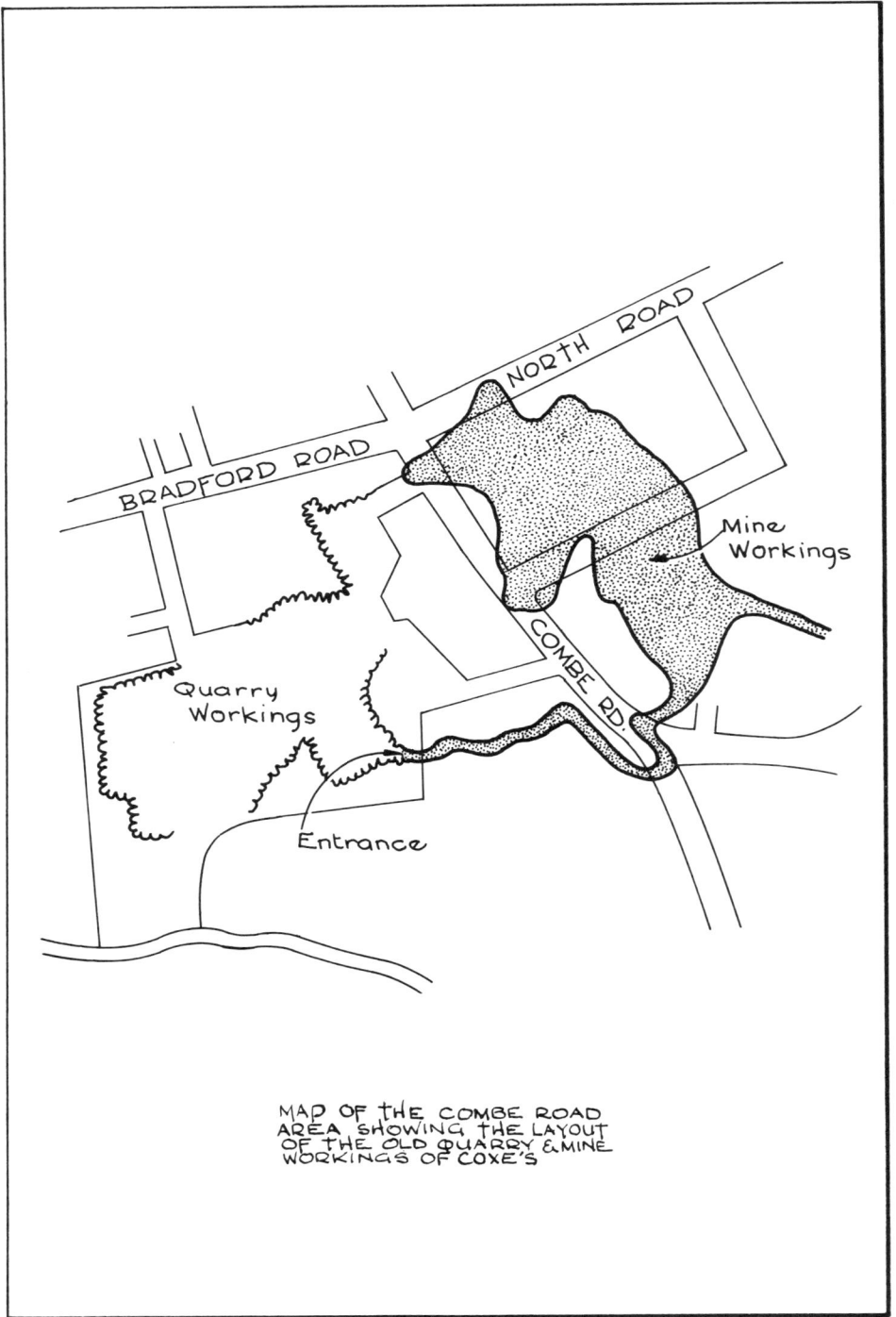

MAP OF THE COMBE ROAD
AREA SHOWING THE LAYOUT
OF THE OLD QUARRY & MINE
WORKINGS OF COXE'S

NORTH ROAD

BRADFORD ROAD

COMBE RD.

Mine Workings

Quarry Workings

Entrance

Plate 26

Further Reading

Historical Guide to Monkton Combe, Combe Down and Claverton	Lee Pitcairn & A. Richardson	1924
Combe Down History	Combe Down TG	1965
Bath Tramways	Colin Maggs	1971
Prior Park	Bryan Little	1975
Bath Freestone Workings	Liz Price	1984
Patrick Y. Alexander	Gordon Cullingham	1985
Holy Trinity Church 1885-1985		1985
Prior Park - A Compleat Landscape	Gillian Clarke	1987

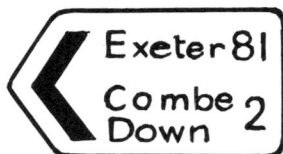

Exeter 81
Combe 2
Down

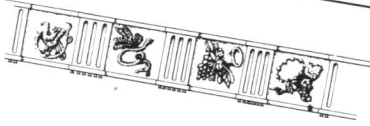

EXPLORING BATH

A new version of a detailed but easy-to-follow guide
to some of the most fascinating landmarks and historic features
of Bath

KEITH DALLIM

EXPLORING BATH

A treasure trove of fascinating information about Bath,
all in an easy-to-follow pictorial presentation
No.2 Centre and East

KEITH DALLIMORE